CONTENTS

SEPTEMBER
Rosh Hashana 3
   Art Activities: Star of David 4
                   Honey-dipped apples 6
                   Foil shofar 8
   Activity Sheets: Secret message 10
                   Festival fill-in 11

OCTOBER
Autumn 12
   Art Activities: Spatter painting 13
                   Pull-along caterpillar 15
                   Straw blowing and sponge painting 17
   Activity Sheets: Autumn acrostic 19
                   Change-a-letter 20

NOVEMBER
Thanksgiving 21
   Art Activities: Mosaic 22
                   Pilgrim boy 24
                   Turkey 26
   Activity Sheets: Circle message 28
                   Scrambled code 29

DECEMBER
Christmas 30
   Art Activities: Ornament 31
                   Tissue wreath 33
                   Lollipop angel 35
   Activity Sheets: Hidden words 37
                   Alphabetical sentences 38

JANUARY
Winter 39
   Art Activities: Colorful snowflakes 40
                   Penguin 42
                   Snowman mobile 44
   Activity Sheets: Crossword code 46
                   Message-gram 47

FEBRUARY
Valentine's Day 48
   Art Activities: Broken heart 49
                   Fabric hearts and flowers 51
                   Weave-a-heart 53
   Activity Sheets: Message in hearts 55
                   Magic word square 56

MARCH

Spring 57
    Art Activities: Tissue butterfly 58
                          Styrofoam flower 60
                          Pinwheels 62
    Activity Sheets: Bifid Cipher code 64
                          Crossword steps 65

APRIL

Easter 66
    Art Activities: Shadow crosses 67
                          Trinket holder 69
                          Easter bonnet 71
    Activity Sheets: Word crosses 73
                          Seek and find 75

MAY

Mother's Day 76
    Art Activities: Vase 77
                          Tissue flower 79
                          Wrapping paper and bow 81
    Activity Sheets: Morse code 83
                          Bible women 84

JUNE

Father's Day 85
    Art Activities: Pencil holder 86
                          Card 88
                          Needlepoint 90
    Activity Sheets: Men of the Bible 92
                          Men in books 93

JULY

Independence Day 94
    Art Activities: Soldier uniform 95
                          Revolutionary reflections 97
                          Soldier 99
    Activity Sheets: Crossword puzzle 101
                          Presidential puzzle 102

AUGUST

Summer 103
    Art Activities: Turtle 104
                          Bee 104
                          Boat mobile 106
    Activity Sheets: Cross-out puzzle 108
                          Sun scramble 109

ANSWER SHEETS 110

September

The Festival of Trumpets:
Mid-September
  is a solemn time. . .
    for worship.
        Leviticus 23:23
        (The Living Bible)

Rosh Hashana

Rosh Hashana, known in biblical times as the Feast of Trumpets, and Yom Kippur, also called the Day of Atonement, are holidays celebrated by the Jews in either September or October, depending upon the lunar calendar. Both of these are regarded as most solemn Jewish holidays.

Rosh Hashana is celebrated as the beginning of a new year. It involves the days of penitence. The beginning of Rosh Hashana is signaled by the blowing of a ram's horn to call the people to repent of their sins. Then prayers are usually said beside a river or lake to mark the washing away of sins. Apples and bread dipped in honey are eaten for a sweet and happy year to follow.

SUBJECT: Rosh Hashana

ART ACTIVITY: Star of David

MATERIALS: Art tissue in varied colors
Polymer medium (high gloss)
  or white glue
Tagboard
Black construction paper
Scissors
Rulers
Brushes
Paint pans or muffin tins

TEACHER PREPARATION: For each child you will need:
1, 9" x 12" piece of tagboard
2, 6" x 8" rectangles of black construction paper
2, 3/4" x 12" black construction paper strips
2, 3/4" x 9" black construction paper strips
Cover work surface with newspapers.

DIRECTIONS: Tear tissue into medium sized irregularly-shaped pieces. Place on tagboard in random design, overlapping colors. When a pleasing design is made, hold pieces in place with left hand and brush over top of tissue with polymer or glue. Cover entire tagboard with tissue and polymer. Set aside to dry. Fold black rectangles in half lengthwise so you have 4" x 6" folded rectangles. Cut 3/4" wide triangles as shown in illustration. Overlap these to make Star of David and glue on tissue collage. Glue strips on edges of collage to form frame. Brush over entire picture with a final coat of polymer or glue.

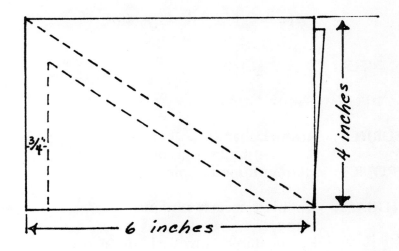

SUBJECT: Rosh Hashana

PROJECT: Honey-dipped apples

MATERIALS: 1 apple for each student
Honey
Knives (table knives will do as they
only need to be sharp enough to
cut apples)
Small paper plates

TEACHER PREPARATION: For very young children, you may want to do the cutting. Otherwise, the children will work in pairs. One will make the "well." The other will cut his apple into wedges to be dipped into the honey.

DIRECTIONS: Cut the top third off of the apple to be made into a well. If the apple is uneven on the bottom, you may need to cut a thin slice off the bottom so apple will stand upright. Cut out core making a well in center of apple. Leave at least 3/8" of apple around sides and on bottom. Fill well with honey. Cut other apple into wedges. Cut off core from each slice. Dip apple wedges into honey and eat. This was done in Jewish homes to assure a "sweet year."

SUBJECT: Rosh Hashana

ART ACTIVITY: Foil shofar (ram's horn)

MATERIALS: For each student you will need:
1, 9" x 12" piece of construction paper in a dark color
Yarn
Foil
Glue
Wide tip felt markers

TEACHER PREPARATION: If desired, make pattern of shofar. Also, you may want to make a sample.

DIRECTIONS: Cut construction paper in half, making two 6" x 9" pieces. Trace or draw shofar on one piece. Cut this out of center of paper. Do not cut rim. This should be a kind of stencil of a shofar. Place stencil on top of other sheet of construction paper. Trace inside stencil so that outline of shofar appears on uncut paper. Remove stencil. Glue yarn on outline of shofar. Then glue yarn across design to divide it into sections (see illustration). Tear or cut piece of foil large enough to cover entire design. Press down around yarn, leaving clear impression of sections. Glue foil onto paper around outside edges of design. Color inside each section with markers. Place stencil over foil shofar and glue in place.

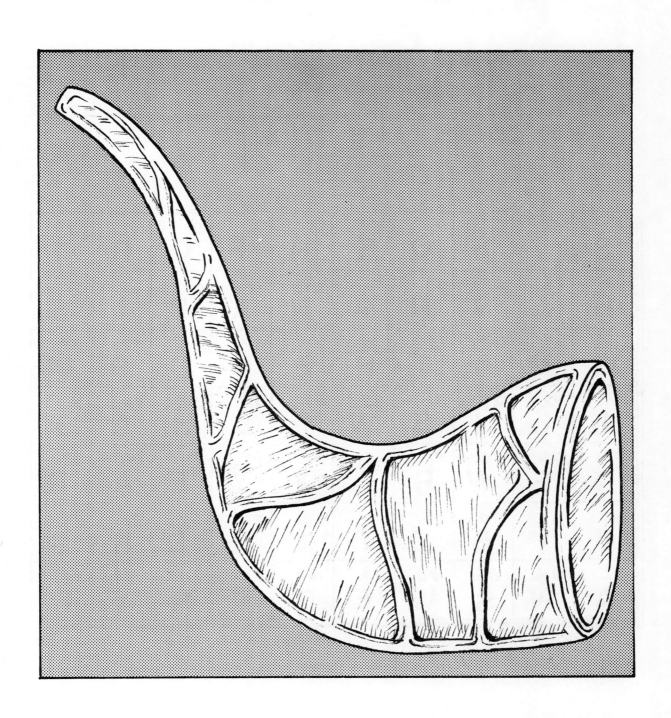

Rosh Hashana #1

DIRECTIONS: Color in all the squares that have even numbers and find the secret message.

2. S	4. T	3. R	7. O	9. S	15. H	6. F	8. O	10. R	12. T
11. H	23. A	25. S	53. H	51. A	49. N	19. A	14. R	1. I	5. S
16. S	18. M	20. A	13. T	17. H	21. E	24. J	26. O	28. R	30. M
40. K	42. L	27. J	31. E	35. W	49. I	55. S	59. H	44. A	46. T
71. N	79. E	83. W	50. R	52. O	54. Y	89. Y	91. E	61. A	63. R
60. B	62. I	70. B	74. O	72. R	68. T	66. L	64. E	92. R	94. S
82. A	84. N	86. S	88. W	90. E	104. R	180. T	200. H	100. E	98. R

10

Rosh Hashana #2

DIRECTIONS: There were 7 festivals that the nation of Israel observed. Can you fill in the blanks to find the names of these festivals? If you are unsure, check Leviticus 23.

— — — — — **F** — — — — —

— — — — **E** — — — —

— — — **S** — — — —

— — — — — — **T** —

I S R A E L

— — — — **V** — — — — — — —

— — — — — — **A** — — — — — —

— — — — — — — **L** — —

October

While the earth remaineth. . .
harvest
shall not cease.

Genesis 8:22

Fall Arrived

I paused amid earth's beauty
To lift my heart in praise,
To thank God for the blessing
of these autumnal days.

Yes, Fall arrived this morning.
I felt her tangy touch
Persuading me to wander
Down paths I love so much.

—Georgia B. Adams

SUBJECT: Autumn

ART ACTIVITY: Spatter painting

MATERIALS: 4" square (approximately) chicken
wire
Toothbrushes
Leaves of various kinds
Orange, yellow, or green tempera
(or any color desired)
White construction paper

TEACHER PREPARATION: Cover working area with newspaper.
It might be a good idea to have old shirts
for younger children. Also, you might want
to cover edges of wire with masking tape.

DIRECTIONS: Arrange leaves on white construction paper. Hold
chicken wire in one hand, over a space not cov-
ered by the leaves. Dip toothbrush in tempera and
then move the bristles back and forth over
chicken wire. When sufficient "spattering" is
done over that spot, move to the next blank space
until all spaces are "spattered." Then very carefully lift leaves and let paper dry.

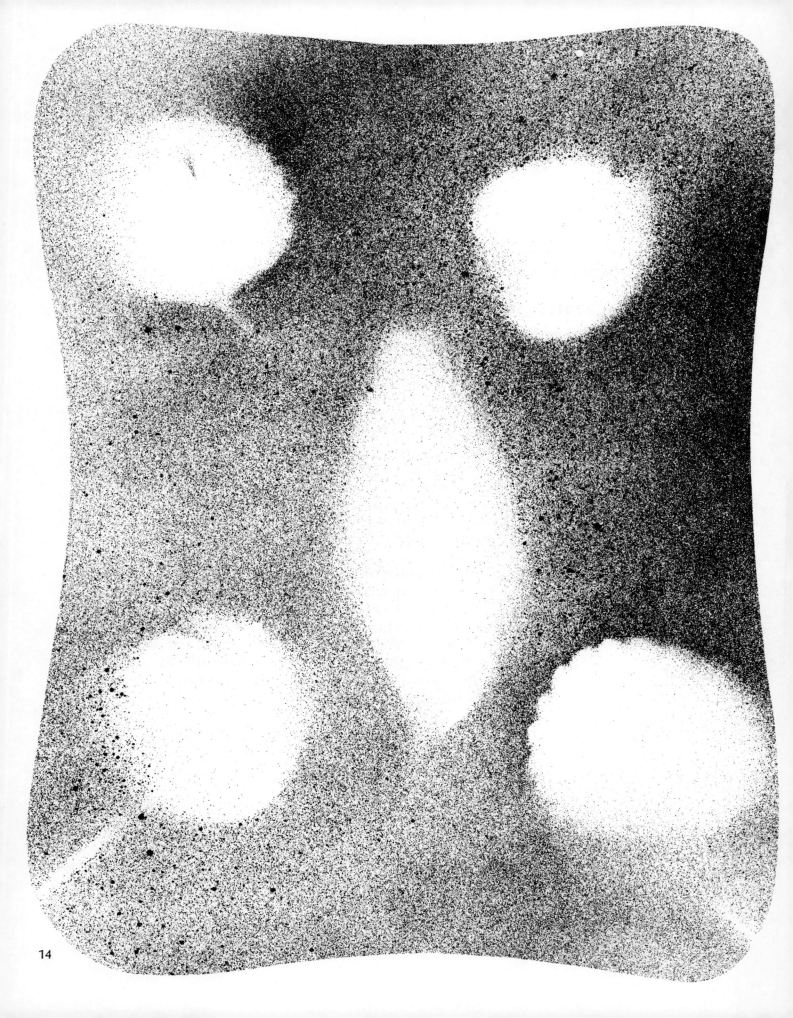

SUBJECT: Autumn

ART ACTIVITY: Pull-along caterpillar

MATERIALS: Paper punch
Green paint
Brushes
Glue
Scissors

TEACHER PREPARATION: For each child you will need:
1 toilet tissue roll
18" yarn or string
construction paper scraps (for eyes, antennae, mouth)

DIRECTIONS: Cut paper tube in half lengthwise and then cut each half into 3 pieces, each about 1 1/2" long (see illustration). Paint outside of pieces green. Cut eyes, antennae, and mouth out of scraps of construction paper. Punch hole in middle of each side of each piece of tubing about 3/8" from bottom. Tie large knot in end of yarn. Thread yarn through holes connecting pieces. The knot is the nose of caterpillar. Glue on eyes and antennae. Tie large knot in yarn at other end of caterpillar and trim off excess yarn.

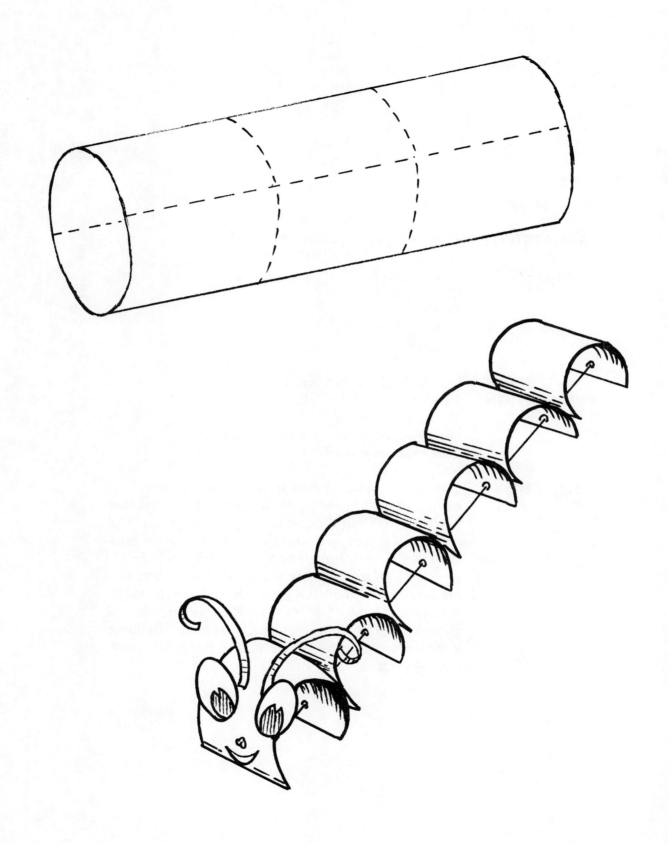

SUBJECT: Autumn

ART ACTIVITY: Straw blowing and sponge painting

MATERIALS: Sponges
White construction paper
Black construction paper (optional)
Black and orange tempera
Straws

TEACHER PREPARATION: For each child provide the following:
1, 1" x 1 1/2" (approximately) sponge
   piece (cut these from ordinary sponges)
1 straw
1, 9" x 12" white construction paper
Black tempera
Orange tempera
Black construction paper if a frame
   is desired.

DIRECTIONS: Instruct children to blow out and not breathe in when blowing on the straw. The straw should not touch the paint. It should be held almost horizontally. Place a few drops of black tempera on the white construction paper, toward the bottom of the paper. Blow hard enough so that the paint spreads in several directions, resembling branches. It is possible that more paint will be needed at specific points. Let dry.

Dip sponge in orange paint and lightly dab on the branches.

Autumn #1

Look up the verses

in the Bible

and find a

key word that

begins with a

letter below. All

the verses are from the

Old Testament and

reveal God's

goodness

to

us.

Psalm 91:11 **A** ___ ___ ___ ___ ___

Proverbs 2:21 **U** ___ ___ ___ ___ ___ ___

Psalm 2:12 **T** ___ ___ ___

Isaiah 41:10 **U** ___ ___ ___ ___ ___

Lamentations 3:22 **M** ___ ___ ___ ___ ___ ___

Psalm 72:12 **N** ___ ___ ___ ___

Autumn #2

DIRECTIONS: When we look forward to the fall season, we usually think of leaves changing colors. See if you can change *fall* into *leaf* in six moves by changing only one letter of the word each move.

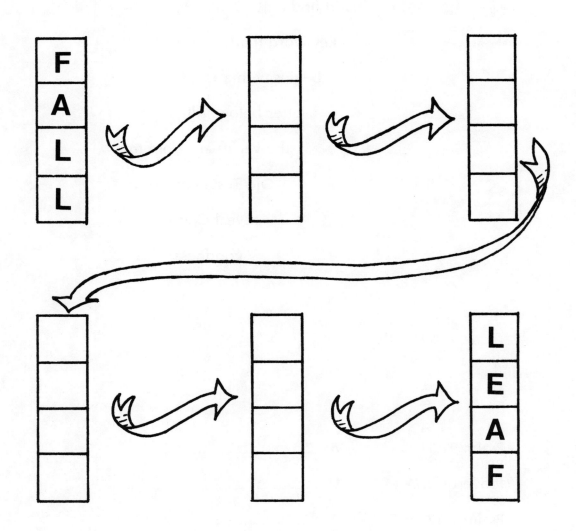

EXAMPLE: Change *dog* to *run* in 5 moves.

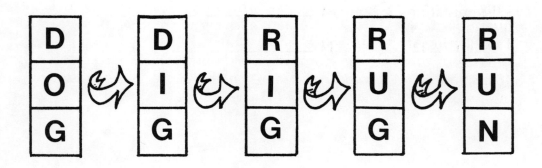

November

Giving
    thanks
always for all things.
       Ephesians 5:20

Thanksgiving

The fourth Thursday of November is a very special day in the United States. It is Thanksgiving—a time for family reunions, bountiful dinners, and reflections on the blessings of the past year.

Thanksgiving goes back to 1620 when the Pilgrims landed on American soil. That first winter was a severe one. The Pilgrims worked hard, but many were not able to complete the building of their homes. Some did not have enough to eat. As a result, only half of the Pilgrims survived. When spring finally came, they worked hard planting their gardens. The Indians were gracious and showed them where to find deer and turkey and how to hunt them. They taught the Pilgrims how to plant corn and catch fish. By summer the gardens were full. There would be plenty when the next winter came around. That fall the Pilgrims had a celebration that lasted for three days. They were able to get wild turkeys, geese, and ducks. From the waters they caught clams, fish, and lobsters. The Indians also brought large quantities of food. Ninety Indians came with their chief Massasoit. The Pilgrims truly had cause to celebrate.

Since that time, the custom has been kept alive, and on October 3, 1863, Abraham Lincoln proclaimed a national day of Thanksgiving.

SUBJECT: Thanksgiving

ART ACTIVITY: Thanksgiving Mosaic

MATERIALS: Construction paper in assorted colors
Glue
Scissors
Styrofoam meat trays or plates
Shellac, varnish, or liquid polymer

TEACHER PREPARATION: It is helpful to have pictures of harvest vegetables, fruits, and flowers and to have made a sample of this project.

DIRECTIONS: Cut piece of construction paper to fit bottom of meat tray and glue down for background. Draw outline of fruits, flowers, and vegetables. Cut pieces in appropriate sizes and shapes and fill in outline. Brush on shellac, varnish or liquid polymer (optional).
NOTE: For a simple project, cut large pieces, like whole flowers or fruit. For a more challenging project, cut small pieces. Either way, try to vary colors and shapes.

SUBJECT: Thanksgiving

ART ACTIVITY: Pilgrim boy

MATERIALS: For each child provide the following:
1, 9" paper plate
1, 6" paper plate
Pink tempera, blue tempera, paintbrush
Black, yellow, and white construction
paper
Black marker, glue, scissors, white crayon
or chalk

TEACHER PREPARATION: Patterns may be dittoed for younger children. A sample should be made to give the older ones an idea of the pilgrim boy to be made.

DIRECTIONS: Paint one side of the large plate blue. Let dry. Paint the smaller plate pink. If white tempera is available, the pink could be diluted. When dry, staple the edge of the smaller plate onto the bigger one to represent the head and body.

From the black construction paper:
Cut hat, the base being approximately
7" across, and 6" high.
Cut rectangle, 2" x 8" for pants. Glue to
the bottom edge of the blue plate to
represent pants. Draw a line down the
middle with white crayon or chalk.
Cut shoes.
Cut bow for collar.

From the white construction paper:
Cut buckle for belt.
Cut a strip and buckle for hat.
Cut collar and sleeves.
Cut circles for white of eyes.

From the yellow construction paper:
Cut hair.

Glue the above pieces in the appropriate places. Use marker to fill in details for eyes and mouth.

SUBJECT: Thanksgiving

ART ACTIVITY: Turkey

MATERIALS: For each child provide the following:
1, 9" paper plate
Dark brown tempera, paintbrush
Marker
Orange, yellow, and beige construction
  paper
Glue

TEACHER PREPARATION: For younger children a pattern may be provided.

DIRECTIONS: Paint one side of the plate dark brown. When dry, make V-shaped cuts around the edge of the plate. Cut a 6" circle from the beige construction paper and glue to lower portion of plate. Cut head and neck from orange construction paper. Cut feet and beak from yellow construction paper. Glue in appropriate places. Use marker to fill in details.

Thanksgiving #1

DIRECTIONS: To find the secret message, start with the letter *w* and write every other letter in the squares in the middle of the circle. Go around the entire circle twice.

Thanksgiving #2

DIRECTIONS: Unscramble the letters in the words below. Write one letter in each square. All the words are related to Thanksgiving. Then arrange the shaded letters to form the missing word.

F W R M Y O A L E

U R Y K E T

L Y P T H M U O

R T V S E H A

S Y A T H D U R

N R L G I O E I

"GIVING __ __ __ __ __ ALWAYS FOR ALL THINGS. . . ."

29

December

*And she shall bring forth
a son, and thou shalt call
his name Jesus; for he
shall save his people from
their sins.*

Matthew 1:21

Christmas

Christmas is a celebration of the birth of Jesus Christ. One cannot be sure how December 25 was established as Christmas, but some have suggested that the date was chosen to correspond to the celebration of the winter solstice by the pagans.

It is interesting to note how some of the customs came into existence. The burning of the Yule log is a custom borrowed from Scandinavian countries where they lighted huge bonfires to celebrate the winter solstice.

The evergreen was honored by the Celtics and the Teutonics as a symbol of eternal life. Legends tell us the crown of thorns Christ wore was made of holly. The berries were supposedly white then, but when the crown of thorns was placed on Christ's head, the blood turned the berries red.

It is believed that the origin of the Christmas tree began with Martin Luther. The sign of an evergreen tree under a star-lit sky impressed him so greatly that he placed a similar tree with lighted candles in his home. Christmas carols are traced back to St. Francis of Assisi, who sang songs of praise to the Christ Child. He is also credited with introducing the Nativity scene.

Santa Claus goes as far back as the fourth century to St. Nicholas who was a bishop in Asia Minor, known for his good works and giving of gifts.

The custom of giving gifts to family members and friends is derived from the three kings who brought gold, frankincense, and myrrh to Jesus Christ at His birth.

SUBJECT: Christmas

ART ACTIVITY: Ornament

MATERIALS: Used Christmas cards (at least 10 per child)
Scissors
Glue

TEACHER PREPARATION: Make for each child a circle and a triangle pattern from cardboard or tagboard (see illustration).

DIRECTIONS: Trace 20 circles on cards. It is easier to draw on the back of the Christmas card pictures because the lines show better. Backs of some cards may be used also if they are brightly colored. Cut out circles. Still working on the backs of the pictures, trace a triangle in center of each circle. Carefully fold circle along lines of triangle with picture on inside of folded triangle. It is important to make points as sharp as possible. Place 5 triangles together in circle pattern with points toward center (see illustration). Glue adjacent "flaps" together. When completely connected, these will form a "beanie cap" shape. Repeat with another 5 triangles. These are the tops and bottoms of your Christmas ball. Place remaining 10 triangles in line with first point up, second point down, third point up, etc. Glue adjacent flaps, then glue ends together forming ring. Glue "caps" on top and bottom. If desired, hole may be punched in one flap and string attached for hanging.

32

SUBJECT: Christmas

ART ACTIVITY: Tissue wreath

MATERIALS: For each student you will need:
1, 9″ paper plate
Glue
Pencil
2″ squares of green tissue
1, 4″ x 24″ red tissue or ribbon

TEACHER PREPARATION: Cut tissue squares.

DIRECTIONS: Cut center out of paper plate. Use the center of the plate to put small puddle of glue on. The rim will form the base for the wreath. Fold a square of tissue around eraser end of pencil. Dip in puddle of glue and attach to rim. Place squares as close together as possible. If desired, make a few red squares to represent berries. Make bow of red tissue. Glue at bottom of wreath.

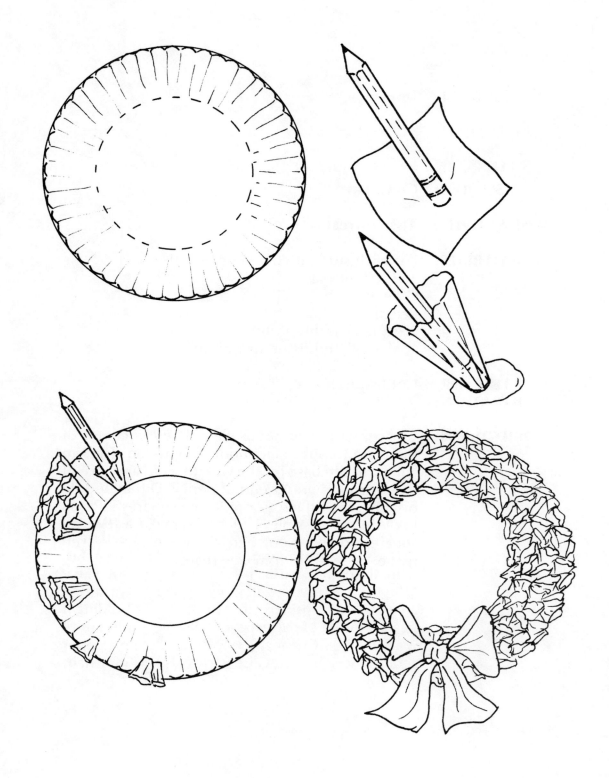

SUBJECT: Christmas

ART ACTIVITY: Lollipop angel

MATERIALS: For each student you will need:
1 round lollipop (red, pink, or orange)
2, 8″ squares of gold foil (wrapping paper is good)
1, 8″ x 14″ white construction paper
1, 14″ x 2″ white construction paper
1, 6″ tube from toilet tissue or paper towels
Scraps of yarn for hair
Scraps of construction paper for eyes and mouth
Glue
Scissors

TEACHER PREPARATION: Make patterns for wings and body.

DIRECTIONS: Cut body from white construction paper. Roll around paper tube to form cone. Glue together in back. Roll 14″ x 2″ strip around body to make arms. Glue onto back. Glue the foil squares together so that gold shows on both sides. Cut wings from this. Glue them in place and curl tips up and out. Place lollipop inside tube and glue it in place by putting a generous amount of glue on stick and holding it against inside of paper tube for a few minutes until partially dry. Cut features of construction paper scraps and glue on. Glue yarn scraps on for hair.

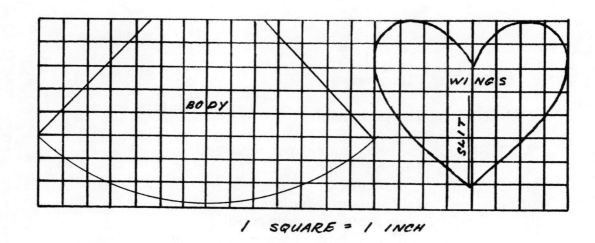

1 SQUARE = 1 INCH

Christmas #1

Hidden in each sentence
below is a word that
relates to Christmas.
Can you find it?

For example: Make a *star* from those sticks.

Answer: EAST

1. Marje sustained those high notes well.

2. Do not mar your desk.

3. Jose phoned me yesterday.

4. Her odd manner bothers me.

5. I never saw Frank incensed like this before.

6. Go sin no more.

7. She exclaimed, "Chris, the roast is burning!"

8. The last armor he had was destroyed in the war.

9. Is that log old?

10. His dog, Shep, herded the cattle into the corral.

Put the following groups of words in alphabetical order.

Example: *loves me Jesus* = Jesus loves me.

1. vile world into our behold uninviting sinful Christ humbly entered.

   _____

   _____

2. came sang hosts angels heavenly.

   _____

3. worship come us let.

   _____

4. our today Savior Christ adore.

   _____

Too easy? Try these by arranging the words in *reverse* alphabetical order.

1. of today Savior welcome all the.

   _____

2. gift you God's received.

   _____

3. born rejoice Son God the of is.

   _____

January

*Thou hast set all the borders
of the earth: thou
hast made. . .
winter.*

Psalms 74:17

Winter Viewpoints

Restful time when the earth slumbers
   'neath the snow,
Hiding all her treasures while frosty
   north winds blow.

A time when woodland creatures have
   need of bounty store,
And yet God watches over them while
   winter's at their door.

Enchanted time for children, as crystal
   flakes of white
Descend to make a wonderland and fill
   hearts with delight.

—Laverne P. Larson

SUBJECT: Winter

ART ACTIVITY: Colorful snowflakes

MATERIALS: For each child you will need:
1, 9″ x 9″ sheet brightly colored paper.
   Origami paper (available in art,
   craft or school supply stores) or foil
   wrapping paper is best.
1, 9″ x 9″ sheet contrasting
   brightly colored paper
1, 9″ x 9″ sheet contrasting brightly
   colored paper
1, 9″ x 12″ sheet of white construction paper
Scissors
Glue

TEACHER PREPARATION: You may want to reproduce directions for cutting and folding. However, the design does not have to be exactly like those shown.

DIRECTIONS: Fold 9″ x 9″ colored paper as shown. Cut as shown in Figure A. Glue on white paper. Fold 9″ x 9″ paper and cut as shown in Figure B. Glue on top of the first snowflake. Fold last 9″ x 9″ paper and cut as shown in Figure C. Glue on top of first two snowflakes.

FOLDING INSTRUCTIONS

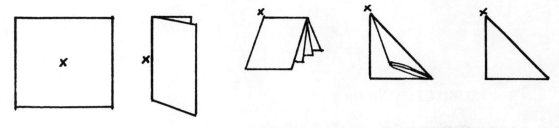

X MARKS THE CENTER OF PAPER

CUTTING INSTRUCTIONS

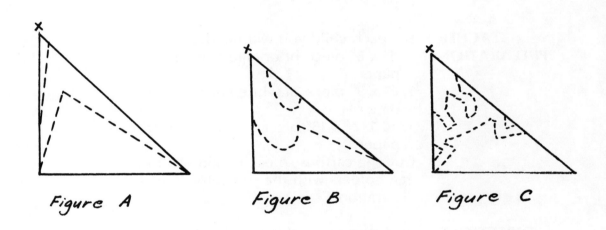

Figure A Figure B Figure C

ASSEMBLING INSTRUCTIONS

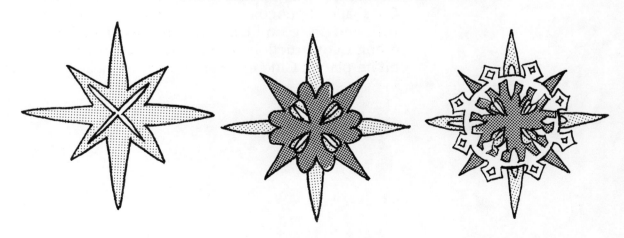

SUBJECT: Winter

ART ACTIVITY: Penguin

MATERIALS: Orange, black, and white construction paper
Scissors
Black Tempera
Jumbo egg cartons
Glue

TEACHER PREPARATION: For each child you will need:
1, 4" x 6" piece of orange construction paper
1, 6" x 9" piece of white construction paper
1, 10 1/2" x 15" piece of black construction paper
Cut egg cartons so each child will have 2 egg holders with the separator (see illustration).

DIRECTIONS: Paint the egg holders white. Paint the separator black as well as the center of the eyes. For younger children, a ditto or pattern may have to be made. Cut shape of penguin from black paper. Cut white vest, and paste on black. Cut bow and feet from orange construction paper and paste in appropriate places. Glue egg carton eyes on head.

SUBJECT: Winter

ART ACTIVITY: Snowman mobile

MATERIALS: White, black, red, brown construction
paper
Yarn or string
Hole punch
Scissors
Glue

TEACHER PREPARATION: For each child you will need:
1, 7" square white construction paper
2, 5" squares white construction paper
1, 3 1/2" square white construction paper
1, 4" x 6" strip black construction paper
1, 4" x 6" strip brown construction paper
1, 4" x 6" strip red construction paper
24" piece of string

DIRECTIONS: Round off the corners of all the squares to make circles.

Cut hat from the 4" x 6" black piece. From scraps of black cut 12 buttons (6 for each side), 2 pairs of eyes, 2 noses, and 2 mouths. Cut branches from brown construction paper. Place one end of each branch between the two 5" white pieces and glue together. Glue 3 buttons on each side of the 5" round white pieces, and 3 buttons on each side of the 7" round piece. Glue eyes, nose and mouth on each side of the 3 1/2" piece. Cut scarf from red piece and glue on bottom of face. From remaining paper cut 2 bands or decorations for hat. Glue band on each side of hat. Punch holes on top and bottom of hat, top and bottom of head, top and bottom of middle piece and top of bottom piece. Cut string into desired lengths and tie snowman together (see illustration).

44

Winter #1

DIRECTIONS: The puzzle below is a verse from the Bible. Each number stands for a letter, beginning with A = 1, B = 2, and so on. When you have figured it out, check Job 37:6 (The Living Bible) to see if you are right.

6.	15.	18.		8.	5.			
4.	9.	18.	5.	3.	20.	19.		
20.	8.	5.		19.	14.	15.	23.	
19.	8.	15.	23.	5.	18.	19.		
1.	14.	4.		19.	20.	15.	18.	13.
	20.	15.		6.	1.	12.	12.	
	21.	16.	15.	14.		20.	8.	5.
			5.	1.	18.	20.	8.	

46

Winter #2

DIRECTIONS: There is a 16-word message for you in this puzzle. Follow each number until you have a word. For example, take number "9." It appears first on line 2 as "H," line 3 as "A," line 5 as "V," and line 6 as "E." Put those letters together and you have the word *have*. Follow each number the same way and write it on the lines below. When you finish, you will have a message from Job 37:15; 38:22.

1	13	4	3	6	7	8	2	5	
D	T	H	K	C	A	N	Y	G	

6	9	3	11	12	13	6	11	14	
O	H	N	V	T	R	N	I	O	

12	7	13	1	9	11	2	11	16	8
H	L	E	O	A	S	O	I	S	A

10	13	7	4	8	15	2	12	16	4
Y	A	L	O	T	T	U	E	N	W

13	11	16	10	9	8	13	5	14	3
S	T	O	O	V	U	U	O	F	O

6	13	8	6	8	9	11	6	13	15
T	R	R	R	E	E	E	O	I	H

11	6	10	13	3	15	5	13	16	6
D	L	U	E	W	E	D	S	W	S

February

*All the special gifts and
powers from God will some-
day come to an end, but
love
goes on forever.*
1 Corinthians 13:8
(The Living Bible)

Valentine's Day

Valentine's Day was originally a Christian festival celebrated in the seventh century to commemorate the martyrdom of Saint Valentine. However, after six or seven hundred years the religious significance was forgotten, and February 14th became a lover's day. In medieval times it was believed that birds began to mate on this day, and that boys and girls followed suit by declaring their romantic intentions with gifts and letters. Today, it is still the custom for lovers of all ages to exchange romantic cards and gifts.

SUBJECT: Valentine's Day

ART ACTIVITY: Broken heart

MATERIALS: For each child provide the following:
1, 12" square white construction paper
1, 9" square red construction paper
Scissors
Glue

TEACHER PREPARATION: Cut squares of construction paper.

DIRECTIONS: Cut heart out of red construction paper. Cut heart apart being very careful to place each piece in the same spot on the white paper as it is cut. When entire heart is cut and placed on white paper, space evenly and glue down.

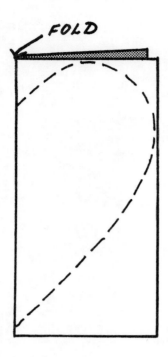
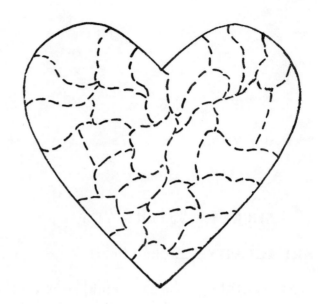

50

SUBJECT: Valentine's Day

ART ACTIVITY: Fabric hearts and flowers

MATERIALS: Construction paper (for pattern)
Fabric with small designs or 3" side
   print ribbon
Fabric or all purpose glue
Covered wire or pipe cleaners
Ball fringe
Florist stick-em
Florist tape
Scissors

TEACHER PREPARATION: If using covered wire, cut into 6"
lengths. Cut fabric or ribbon into
9" strips.

DIRECTIONS: Step 1: Make heart pattern about 2 1/2" long out of construction paper.

Step 2: Trace hearts onto fabric.

Step 3: Glue wire around hearts leaving one end long.

Step 4: Trim fabric from around heart. Twist short end of wire around long wire at point of heart.

Step 5: Gather 6 hearts around one ball from fringe. Secure these with stick-em. Wrap florist tape around bottom of flower and stem.

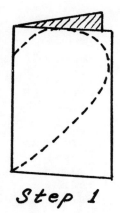
Step 1

Step 2

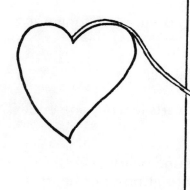
Step 3

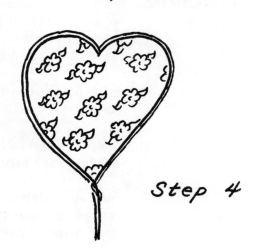
Step 4

Step 5

SUBJECT: Valentine's Day

ART ACTIVITY: Weave-a-heart

MATERIALS: For each child provide the following:
1, 8" x 12" sheet lavender construction paper
1, 6" x 8" sheet pink construction paper
1, 6" x 8" sheet white construction paper
Scissors
Glue

TEACHER PREPARATION: Cut white paper into 1 1/2" x 8" strips or narrower widths if desired. For younger children, fold the pink construction paper in half lengthwise. Fold each side in 1/2" as a cutting guide. Unfold. Fold paper in half breadthwise, fold in half again and again.

DIRECTIONS: Fold pink construction paper in half lengthwise. Then fold sides over 1/2". If folds have been made for the child breadthwise, the child cuts on the lines to the folded edge. Weave the white strips in and out of the pink construction paper.

Fold the 8" x 12" lavender construction paper in half for card. Trace or draw a reasonably big heart on the front. Then, beginning in the middle of the heart, the child cuts the heart shape out of the lavender paper. Make sure the edges are intact because the lavender template with the shape cut out is the part to be used. Now glue the woven sheet on the back of the lavender template. On the other side the child can write a verse for Valentine's Day.

Valentine #1

DIRECTIONS: Color in the triangles that have a heart and you'll find a word that is important not only on Valentine's Day but on every day of the year.

Valentine #2

DIRECTIONS: With the help of the clues given below, fill in the correct words in the boxes. If your answers are correct, each word will appear twice in the box, once across and once down. The first word in each puzzle has to do with Valentine's Day.

1. Fondness
2. Opposite of close
3. To sell
4. Finishes

1. To be nice to someone
2. A thought
3. To be close to
4. To be brave

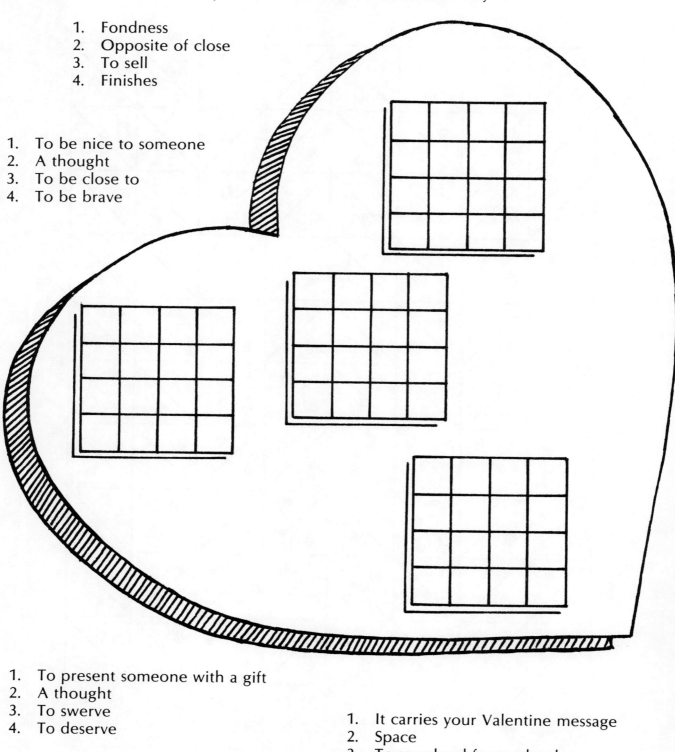

1. To present someone with a gift
2. A thought
3. To swerve
4. To deserve

1. It carries your Valentine message
2. Space
3. To say aloud from a book
4. Opposite of Mom's

56

March

Ask the Lord for rain
in the
springtime
and he will
answer. . . .
Zechariah 10:1
(The Living Bible)

Spring

Close to my heart I fold each lovely
   thing
The sweet day yields; and not discon-
   solate
With calm impatience of the woods, I
   wait
For leaf and blossom, when God gives
   us Spring.

—John Greenleaf Whittier

SUBJECT: Spring

ART ACTIVITY: Tissue butterfly

MATERIALS: Scissors
Glue
Colored tissue paper
Polymer medium (gloss finish) or
white glue (thinned a little with
water)
Brushes
Strips of construction paper or
pipe cleaners (optional)

TEACHER PREPARATION: For each child you will need:
2, 9" x 9" squares black construction
paper
2, 9" x 1 1/2" strips black construction
paper (or 9" x 3" strip folded)
Pattern for butterfly, if desired.
(Older children can probably cut
these without a pattern)
1, 9" x 9" sheet of tissue in a pastel
color

DIRECTIONS: Place 2 black squares on top of each other and fold in the middle. Cut outline of butterfly as shown in illustration. Unfold and spread one outline on newspaper-covered working surface. Glue tissue sheet on top of butterfly. Tear or cut other pieces of contrasting tissue and place them on tissue. Brush over them with polymer or glue. This will make a tissue collage. When a pleasing pattern has been made, glue other butterfly on top of tissue. Trim edges of tissue to fit butterfly. Round edges of 1 1/2" strips of black. Glue these on bottom and top for butterfly bodies. Antennae may be added from strips of construction paper or pipe cleaners.

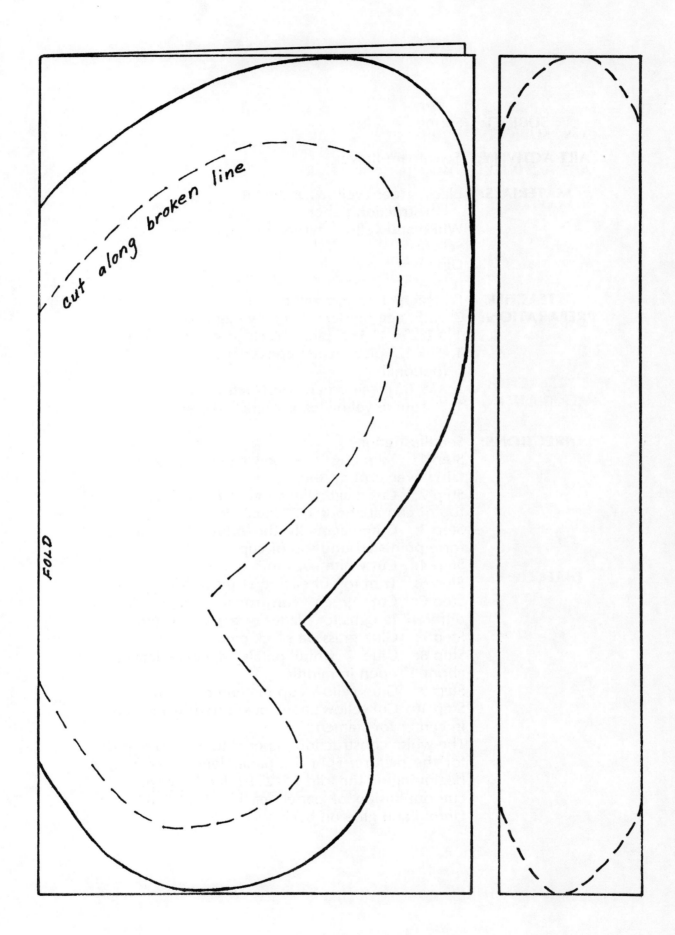

SUBJECT: Spring

ART ACTIVITY: Styrofoam flower

MATERIALS: Black, green, yellow, and white
   construction paper
White and yellow styrofoam egg cartons
Scissors
Glue

TEACHER PREPARATION: For each child you will need:
2 white egg holders, 1 yellow egg holder
1, 8 1/2″ x 11 1/2″ piece black construction paper
1, 9″ x 12″ piece white construction paper
   (optional)
1, 4″ x 8″ piece green construction paper
1, 1″ square yellow construction paper

DIRECTIONS: See illustrations.
Step 1:   Trim edge of yellow egg cup so that it is fairly even around the top.
Step 2:   Cut diagonally about 3/8″ deep around top of cup at about 1/2″ intervals.
Step 3:   Cut diagonally the other direction to form points around top of cup.
Step 4:   Cut white cups into quarters.
Step 5:   Trim top of each quarter to form petal.
Step 6:   Cut green construction paper into different lengths for blades of grass and stem.
Step 7:   Glue grass on black paper.
Step 8:   Glue 7 white petals in circle leaving about 1″ open in middle.
Step 9:   Glue yellow cup in center of petals.
Step 10: Cut yellow paper into thin strips and glue in center for stamens.
The white construction paper is to make a frame for the picture. Fold the paper lengthwise and, beginning on the fold 1 1/2″ from edge of paper, cut out inside of paper leaving 1 1/2″ frame. Unfold and glue on back.

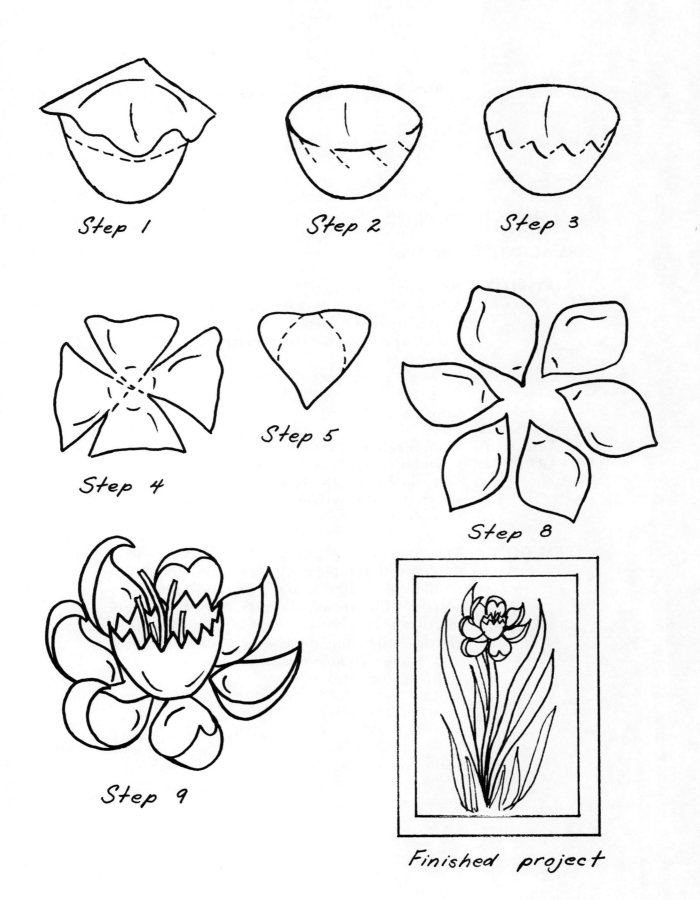

SUBJECT: Spring

ART ACTIVITY: Pinwheels

MATERIALS: For each child you will need:
1, 4" to 6" square of tagboard or heavy construction paper
1 unsharpened pencil with eraser or wood dowel
1 straight pin or tack
Scissors
Crayons or markers

TEACHER PREPARATION: Mark diagonals on each square as shown in illustration, leaving 1" unmarked in center. (Older students can do this themselves.) Mark arrows on corners to be folded.

DIRECTIONS: Cut along lines, stopping 1/2" on each side from the center. Decorate both sides of the paper, using a different design on the front and back. Bring corners with arrows to center. Stick pin or tack through all four corners and the pinwheel center. Place pencil behind pinwheel and stick pin or tack into eraser. (Teacher may do the pinning for younger students.)

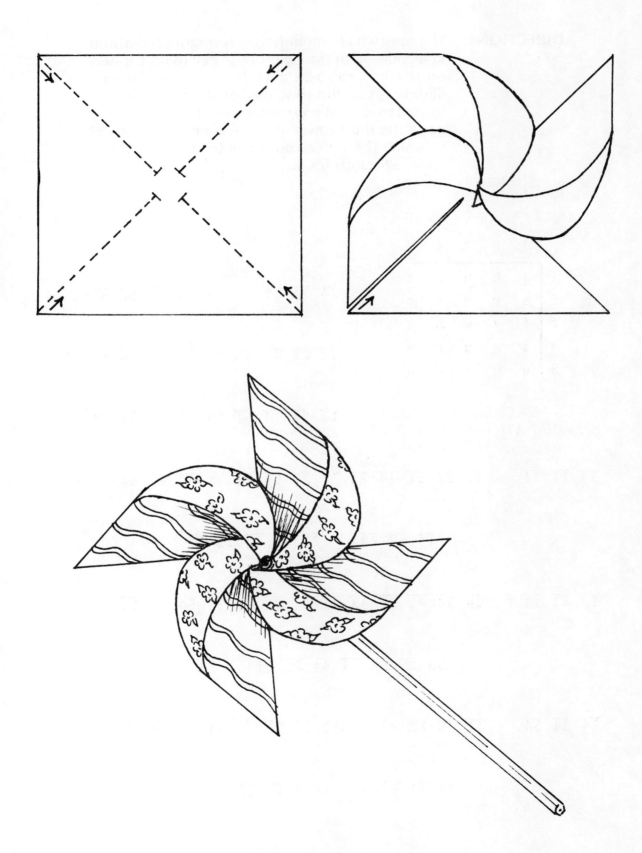

63

Spring #1

DIRECTIONS: The song which reminds us of springtime is written in a code. With the help of the key (Bifid Cipher) on the left, can you decode the song? The first digit tells you the row; the second digit tells you the column. So if you want to find the letter for 32, go to the third row and move over to the second column. The letter you come to is a v so, in this code, 32 stands for v.

	1	2	3	4	5
1	l	b	q	a	c
2	s	r	d	t	o
3	f	v	m	h	w
4	i	x	g	k	y
5	u	n	z	e	p

$\overline{14}\ \overline{11}\ \overline{11}$ $\overline{24}\ \overline{34}\ \overline{41}\ \overline{52}\ \overline{43}\ \overline{21}$

$\overline{12}\ \overline{22}\ \overline{41}\ \overline{43}\ \overline{34}\ \overline{24}$ $\overline{14}\ \overline{52}\ \overline{23}$

$\overline{12}\ \overline{54}\ \overline{14}\ \overline{51}\ \overline{24}\ \overline{41}\ \overline{31}\ \overline{51}\ \overline{11}$'

$\overline{14}\ \overline{11}\ \overline{11}$ $\overline{15}\ \overline{22}\ \overline{54}\ \overline{14}\ \overline{24}\ \overline{51}\ \overline{22}\ \overline{54}\ \overline{21}$ $\overline{43}\ \overline{22}\ \overline{54}\ \overline{14}\ \overline{24}$

$\overline{14}\ \overline{52}\ \overline{23}$ $\overline{21}\ \overline{33}\ \overline{14}\ \overline{11}\ \overline{11}$'

$\overline{14}\ \overline{11}\ \overline{11}$ $\overline{24}\ \overline{34}\ \overline{41}\ \overline{52}\ \overline{43}\ \overline{21}$ $\overline{35}\ \overline{41}\ \overline{21}\ \overline{54}$ $\overline{14}\ \overline{52}\ \overline{23}$

$\overline{35}\ \overline{25}\ \overline{52}\ \overline{23}\ \overline{54}\ \overline{22}\ \overline{31}\ \overline{51}\ \overline{11}$'

$\overline{24}\ \overline{34}\ \overline{54}$ $\overline{11}\ \overline{25}\ \overline{22}\ \overline{23}$ $\overline{43}\ \overline{25}\ \overline{23}$ $\overline{33}\ \overline{14}\ \overline{23}\ \overline{54}$

$\overline{24}\ \overline{34}\ \overline{54}\ \overline{33}$ $\overline{14}\ \overline{11}\ \overline{11}$.

64

Spring #2

What do you think of when we say spring?

See if you can fill in the steps with the help of the "spring" clues.

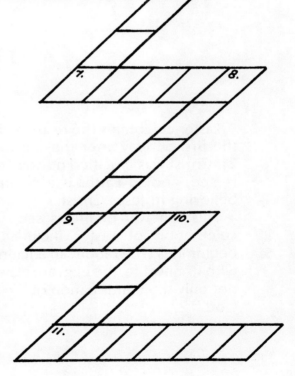

ACROSS

1. The season that officially begins March 21
3. A bird
5. Freshness
7. This becomes green in the spring
9. This garden must have looked like spring all year
11. A bird

DOWN

2. During spring all plant life seems to ___ ___ ___ ___
4. We get a lot of this during the spring
6. We hear birds sing their ___ ___ ___
8. Another word for *picture*
10. A bird's home

*He is not here, but
is risen. . . .*
Luke 24:6

Easter

Easter celebrates the resurrection of Jesus Christ. It is observed on the first Sunday after the full moon that comes on or after March 21. Christ was crucified during Passover, and in three days He resurrected, and so Easter is a celebration of new life shared by those believing in Jesus Christ.

This renewal of life is seen in all of God's creation, and the celebration of Easter includes many symbols of nature's new beginnings. The rabbit, an ancient symbol of fertility, and the chicken with its new life, the egg, are especially popular. The lamb symbolizes not only the continuation of life for the sheep but also the "Lamb of God."

SUBJECT: Easter

ART ACTIVITY: Shadow crosses

MATERIALS: For each student you will need:
3, 3" x 5" pieces of black construction paper
1, 3" x 5" piece white construction paper
1, 9" x 12" piece Manila paper
Watercolors or tempera paint thinned with water
Brushes
Scissors

TEACHER PREPARATION: Cover working area with newspaper. If desired, you may make patterns for crosses.

DIRECTIONS: Brush over Manila paper with clear water and before paper dries, paint background with watercolors or thinned tempera. Do not use pencil or dark outlines. This should be more of a suggested background rather than a detailed picture. The wet paper will produce a misty effect. Make sure entire sheet of Manila is painted. While this dries, cut 3 black crosses and 1 white cross. Place 2 black crosses on the paper with the white cross between them. Glue these down. Place remaining black cross slightly in front of the white cross so that the white cross creates a "shadow" effect. Glue the black cross in position.

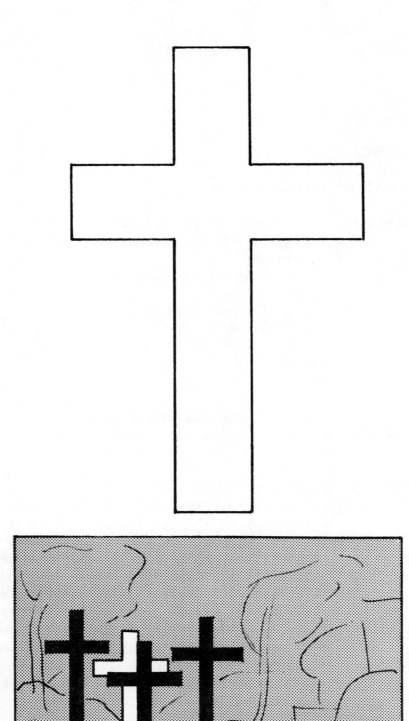

SUBJECT: Easter

ART ACTIVITY: Trinket holder

MATERIALS: Yellow styrofoam egg cartons
Black construction paper
Blue and orange felt
Movable eyes (optional, available from
craft stores)
Tiny artificial flowers (optional)
Glue
Scissors
Stapler

TEACHER PREPARATION: For each child you will need:
1 1/2 yellow styrofoam egg carton
3" x 5" piece black construction paper
1 pair movable eyes (optional)
1 sprig of artificial flowers (optional)
1, 6" x 9" piece orange felt
1, 3" square blue felt

DIRECTIONS: Cut tops off both egg cartons. These will not be used. Cut one bottom in half, lengthwise, so that you have 6 egg cups intact. Invert this strip and staple onto other carton. These are the heads of the ducklings. Cut orange felt into webbed feet and glue on bottoms of egg cups. Cut 1 1/2" strips of orange felt. Round off the ends. Then, with the scissor points in the middle of each strip, insert into each egg cup for the bill. Cut eyes from blue felt and glue. If desired, glue movable eyes on the last duck—"Mother Duck" and also glue sprig of flowers on top. Cut 1" strips from black construction paper, fringe edges, and glue on top of each head.

69

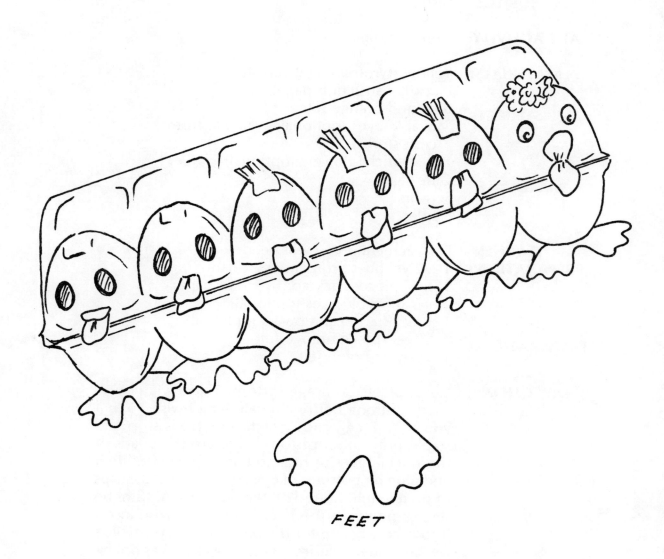

FEET

SUBJECT: Easter

ART ACTIVITY: Easter bonnet

MATERIALS: For each child you will need:
1, 12" x 18" piece white or yellow
    construction paper
Scraps of different colored
    construction paper
Scissors
Glue

TEACHER PREPARATION: You may want to make a sample for the children.

DIRECTIONS: Make a cut, approximately 7" long, from each corner into the center. Overlap the two points over the "triangle" and staple (see illustration). Do the same to the other end. If desired, curl corners back. Decorate with flowers, bunnies, etc.

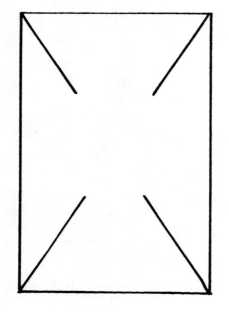
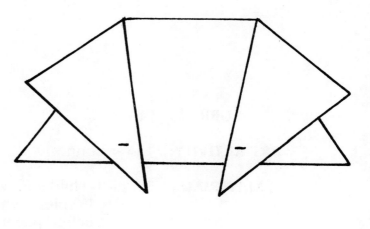
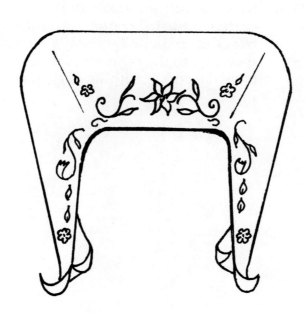

Easter #1

DIRECTIONS: From the clues given, can you fill in the horizontal word that corresponds to the vertical?

1. On EASTER morning the angel said, "He is not here, for He is _____ .
2. One of the disciples on the EMMAUS road was _____ .
3. What PETER did that broke the heart of Jesus.
4. What JOSEPH of Arimathea gave to Jesus at His death.
5. One of the WOMEN to go to the grave was _____ .
6. The person to whom the angel said, "Why are you crying?"
7. Jesus died on the day of PASSOVER; He arose on the morning of the _____ .
8. NICODEMUS brought _____ to embalm Jesus.
9. The first people to visit the tomb on Sunday MORNING were _____ .
10. What happened to the STONE that was at the entrance of the tomb?
11. In exchange for Jesus, the Jews wanted BARABBAS, who was a _____ .
12. Simon, the CYRENIAN, carried the _____ for Jesus.

```
1.        E                2.   _ _ E _ _ _ _
          A                         M
     _ _  S  _ _                    M
          T                         A
          E                         U
          R                         S


              3.      P
                 _  E _ _ _ _
                      T
                      E
                      R
```

73

4.   J   5.   W   6.   _ A _ _
   _ O _ _   _ O _ _ _   N
     S   M   G
     E   E   E
     P   N   L
     H

7.   P   8. _ _ N _ _ _ _ _   9. _ _ M _ _
   _ A _ _ _ _ _   I   O
     S   C   R
     S   O   N
     O   D   I
     V   E   N
     E   M   G
     R   U
                      S

10. S   11.   B   12.   C
   _ O _ _ _   A   Y
     N   R   _ R _ _ _
     E   A   E
                    _ _ B _ _ _   N
                    B   I
                    A   A
                    S   N

Easter #2

Seek and find the following verse:

He is not here, but is risen!
Remember how he spoke. . . .
Luke 24:6

The words are spelled forwards, backwards, across, down and diagonally! (The words *he* and *is* are repeated twice in the puzzle also.)

H	N	O	T	R	F	E	R	E	H
O	E	G	A	I	S	B	S	T	E
W	S	R	L	W	T	P	U	O	N
H	J	I	K	N	O	I	Z	T	W
S	I	S	M	K	L	P	L	S	U
T	F	E	G	A	L	I	L	E	E
O	E	N	G	E	K	O	P	S	M
B	D	R	E	M	E	M	B	E	R

75

May

*Who can find a virtuous
woman? . . .Her children
rise up and call her
blessed.*

Proverbs 31:1, 28

Mother's Day

Mother's Day is celebrated on the second Sunday in May. It is a day set aside to honor all mothers. Anna M. Jarvis, a native of Grafton, West Virginia, is credited with starting this tradition. On May 9, 1906, on the first anniversary of her mother's death she held a memorial meeting with friends, and in 1907 a church service was held on that date. As a result of her efforts, Philadelphia observed May 10, 1908, as Mother's Day. Miss Jarvis continued her efforts by writing to many influential people to observe that day. In May, 1913, Pennsylvania made it a state holiday. In 1913 the United States Congress recommended that the second Sunday in May be made a national holiday honoring mothers.

SUBJECT: Mother's Day

ART ACTIVITY: Vase

MATERIALS: 1 empty bottle for each child
(salad dressing, syrup, pop bottles
with interesting shapes are good)
Windex in spray bottle
Aquarium paint (available from pet
or hobby shops)
Brushes
Newspaper

TEACHER PREPARATION: Cover work surface with papers.
Make sure bottles are clean and
dry.

DIRECTIONS: Spray bottles thoroughly on outside with Windex.
Allow to dry. Paint with aquarium paint. Paint will
crackle and form "frosted" texture. Allow to dry
thoroughly.

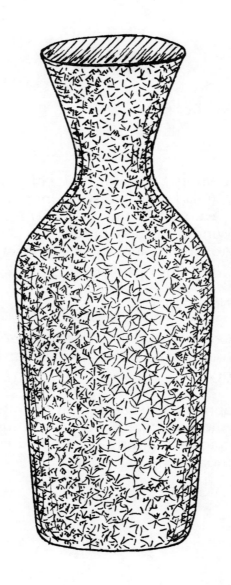

SUBJECT: Mother's Day

ART ACTIVITY: Tissue flower

MATERIALS: Scissors
Floral wire
Pink tissue

TEACHER PREPARATION: For each child provide the following:
6, 8 1/2" x 13" pieces pink tissue
Depending on how long the vase is,
cut wire accordingly, adding
approximately 3" to the length
of the vase.

DIRECTIONS: Keeping all 6 sheets of tissue together, fold in accordian-like fashion breadthwise, in approximately 1" folds. If desired, trim corners off ends to make rounded "petals." After all folds have been gathered into one, use floral wire to tie in center. Bend wire over 2". Use excess wire to twist and secure the folds. Carefully separating each sheet, bring each one up to the center. Do this for both sides.

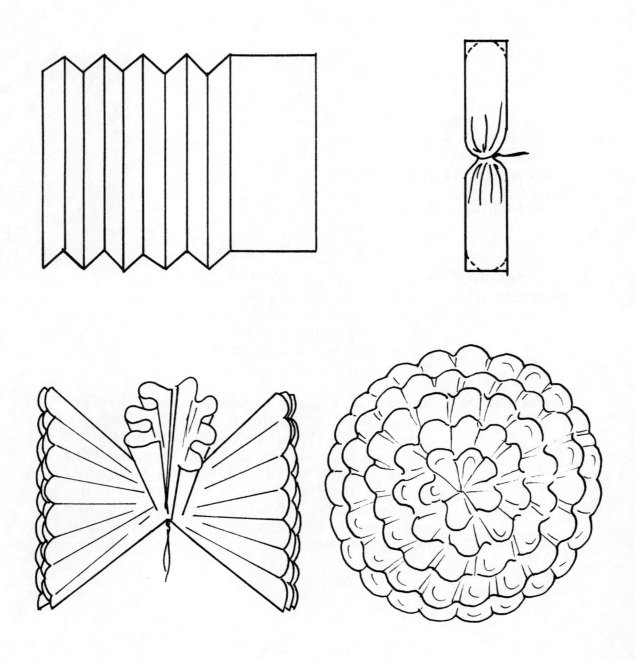

SUBJECT: Mother's Day

ART ACTIVITY: Wrapping paper and bow

MATERIALS: White tissue paper
Pink and green tempera
Sponge pieces (cut from regular sponges)
1 1/4" wide "Tie Tie" ribbon or any ribbon
    that sticks to itself when moistened
Scissors

TEACHER PREPARATION: For each child you will need:
1 piece of white tissue large enough
    to wrap Mother's gift
2 sponge pieces
1, 6" long ribbon, 1 1/4" wide
1, 8" long ribbon, 1 1/4" wide
1, 10" long ribbon, 1 1/4" wide

DIRECTIONS: Fold 6" strip in half, and press on fold so crease shows. Unfold. This will mark the center of each strip. Tear strip into 4 equal strips. Place strips as shown in illustration. Moisten and attach in center. Bring ends of each strip together. Moisten and attach. This will form a ball with strips of ribbon evenly spaced. Moisten the inside top and bottom of the ball. Hold the top and twist slightly to the right and stick top and bottom together (press and hold for a few seconds) making a bow.

Follow same procedure with 8" and 10" strips.

Moisten centers and stick 8" bow on 10" and the 6" on the 8". The 6" bow might be difficult for younger children to manipulate.

Wrapping paper: Dip end of sponge in pink tempera and dab lightly on tissue. Then dip sponge in green tempera and dab lightly on tissue. Let dry.

82

Mother's Day #1

DIRECTIONS: The verse below is in Morse code. See if you can find out what it says. (One word on each line)

"..·   ····   ··   ——   —··   ·   ·   ··   ·   —·,

·   ·   —···   ·   ··   ··

··   ··   ·   ·   ··—   ··

·····   ·—   ··   ·   —·   —   ···"

A = . __		N = __ .
B = __ . . .		O = . .
C = .. .		P = ...
D = __ ..		Q = .. __ .
E = .		R = . ..
F = . __ .		S = ...
G = __ __ .		T = __
H = ...		U = .. __
I = ..		V = ... __
J = __ . __ .		W = . __ __
K = __ . __		X = . __ ..
L = ___		Y = ...
M = __ __		Z = ...

83

Mother's Day #2

DIRECTIONS: We have some famous women in the Bible. Write their names in the blanks. The first letter of each will spell MOTHER.

M ___ ___ ___

O ___ ___ ___ ___

T ___ ___ ___ ___ ___ ___

H ___ ___ ___ ___ ___

E ___ ___

R ___ ___ ___ ___ ___

Clues:

1. The mother of Jesus

2. The sister of Ruth

3. A very kind woman whose name is also Dorcas
4. Mother of Samuel

5. First mother

6. Mother of Joseph

June

Honor
thy
father. . . .

Exodus 20:12

Father's Day

Father's Day is celebrated on the third Sunday of June. The observance of this day can be credited to Mrs. John Bruce Dodd, who in 1909 persuaded the Ministerial Society of Spokane, Washington, to honor fathers with special church services. The idea was officially approved by President Woodrow Wilson in 1916, and in 1924 President Calvin Coolidge recommended national observance of the occasion "to establish more intimate relations between fathers and their children, and to impress upon fathers the full measure of their obligations."

SUBJECT: Father's Day

ART ACTIVITY: Pencil holder

MATERIALS: Small juice cans
Macaroni and noodles in varied
  shapes
Glue
Spray paint (gold is especially pretty)
Masking tape

TEACHER PREPARATION: Cover working area with papers.
Make sure cans are clean and dry.
If top edges are sharp, cover with
masking tape. Put noodles in piles
so that a variety of shapes are
easily accessible to all students.

DIRECTIONS: Glue noodles on cans in any desired pattern. Hold each noodle for a few seconds to allow the glue to harden slightly. When entire can is covered, spray with paint. (Be sure to spray paint in a well-ventilated area or outdoors.)

SUBJECT: Father's Day

ART ACTIVITY: Card

MATERIALS: For each child you will need:
1, 7" x 18" piece orange construction paper
1, 3" x 7" piece blue construction paper
Scissors
Glue

DIRECTIONS: Fold 7" x 18" orange construction paper in half to make 7" x 9" rectangle. About 1 3/4" below the fold make a cut 1 1/2" long on both sides. Fold the tops down to make a collar. Make a tie from blue paper. Glue in center. Then glue collar down. Write appropriate message inside card.

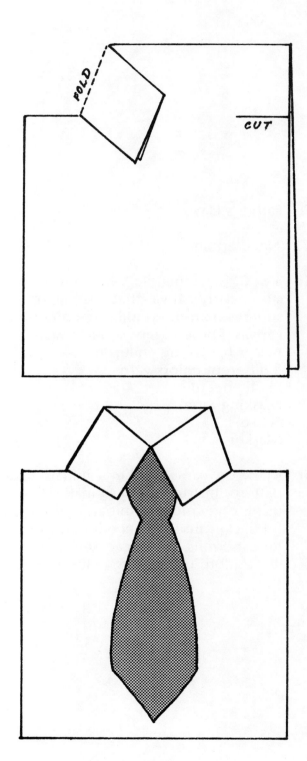

SUBJECT: Father's Day

ART ACTIVITY: Needlepoint

MATERIALS: 4" x 6" piece needlepoint canvas. Some stores carry canvas that has bigger squares than the regular needlepoint canvas. These bigger squares work better for young children.
2 different colors yarn
Plastic needle
Masking tape
Scissors
Marker

DIRECTIONS: Mark on canvas father's initials or any desired pattern. Instruct pupil to make diagonal stitches, using one color for initials and contrasting color for background. Cover edges with masking tape. If time permits, pupil can sew around edges (see illustration) using same color as initials.

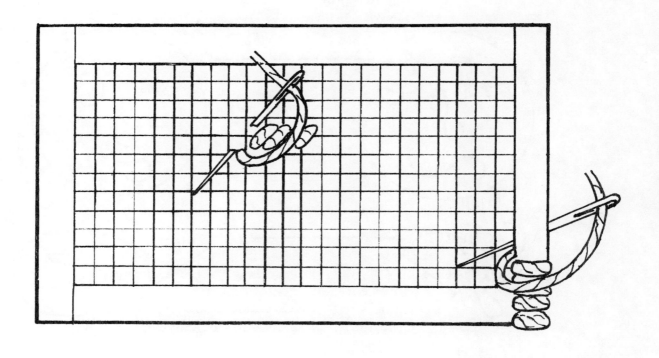

DIRECTIONS: Have fun trying to figure out the names of ten men in the Bible. Each picture has all the letters of the man's name.

Father's Day #1

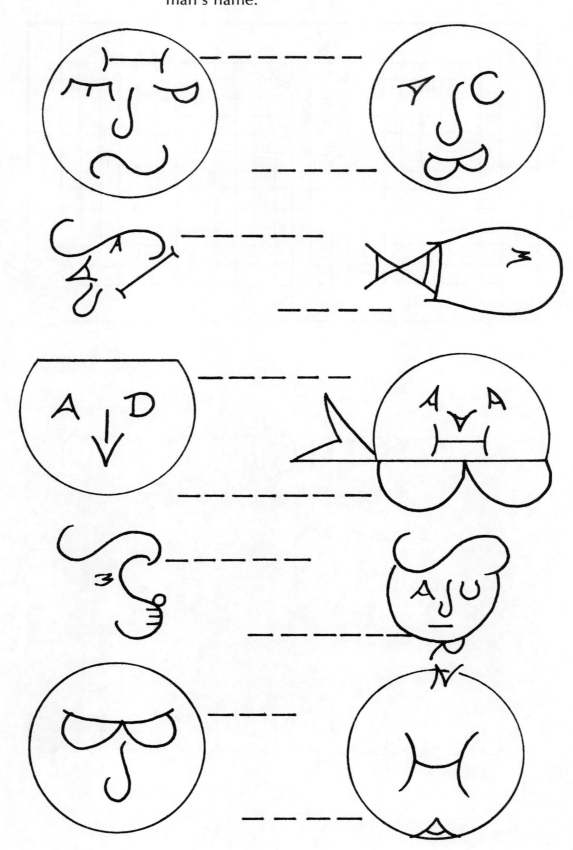

Father's Day #2

DIRECTIONS: Fill in the blanks with the name of a man, and you will have a book of the Bible.

1. __ __ __ __ S I S

2. __ __ __ __ U A

3. __ __ __ U E L

4. __ __ __ I E L

5. __ __ __ O T H Y

6. __ __ __ A H

7. E C C __ __ __ I A S T E S

8. __ __ __ L

9. D E U T E __ __ __ O M Y

10. __ __ __ __ __ __ P I A N S

93

July

I exhort, therefore, that first of all, prayers
. . .be made. . .for kings, and for all that
are in authority. . . .

1 Timothy 2:1, 2

Independence Day

Independence Day is one of the chief legal holidays in the United States. It commemorates the formal adoption of the Declaration of Independence by the Continental Congress in Philadelphia on July 4, 1776. On that day, the document was approved by the delegates, and the President of the Congress, John Hancock, made it official with his signature. Parades, fireworks, and family outings are part of the celebrations each year.

SUBJECT: Patriotic

ART ACTIVITY: Soldier uniform

MATERIALS: 1 large grocery bag
1 lunch bag
Green tempera
2" x 12" piece black construction paper
6" x 14" piece black construction paper
2 1/2" x 3" piece yellow construction paper
9" x 12" piece white construction paper
Scissors
Glue
Paintbrushes
Crayons

DIRECTIONS: Paint front side of grocery bag green. Let dry. Cut buttons and buckle from yellow paper. Trace pupil's hands on white paper and cut out. Cut patches from white construction paper and color.

Cut 6" x 14" black paper into 1" x 6" strips. Fringe one edge of every strip and glue on small bag for hat. The strips should be glued on so that the fringed edge is toward the open end of the bag.

Glue black belt, buckle, hands, buttons, and patches on large bag in appropriate places. Cut slit in bottom of bag so it can be slipped over head and worn as uniform.

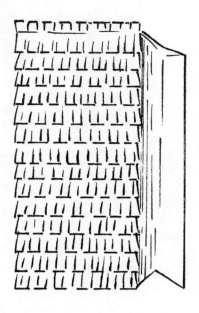
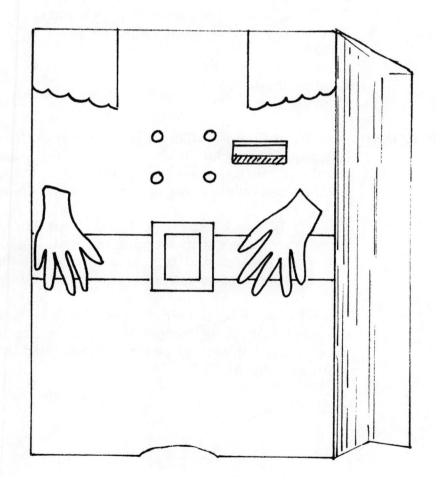

SUBJECT: 4th of July (or Patriotic)

ART ACTIVITY: Revolutionary reflections

MATERIALS: For each child you will need:
1, 9" x 12" piece white construction paper
1, 4" x 4" piece navy blue construction paper
1, 4" x 4" piece red construction paper
1, 9" x 3/4" navy construction paper strip
1, 9" x 3/4" red construction paper strip
1, 12" x 3/4" navy construction paper strip
1, 12" x 3/4" red construction paper strip
Scissors
Glue

DIRECTIONS: Fold red 4" square in half. Using the fold as the bottom, draw a 2" tall *1* and *7*. Cut out numerals, leaving paper folded. Fold navy 4" square in half. Using the fold as the bottom, draw a 2" tall *7* and *6*. Cut out numerals, leaving paper folded. Unfold numerals. Arrange and glue in center of white paper, using red *1*, navy *7*, red *7*, navy *6*. Glue strips on edges of white to form frame.

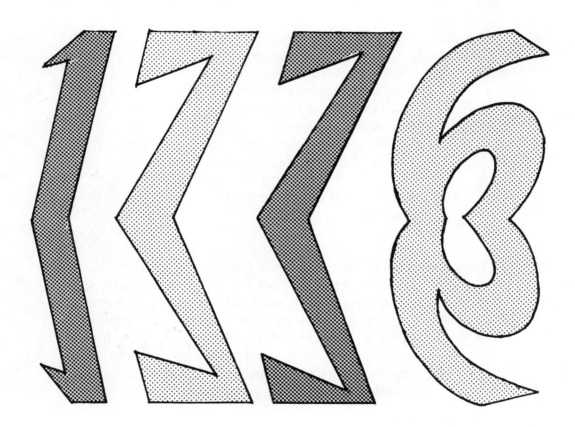

SUBJECT: Patriotic

ART ACTIVITY: Soldier

MATERIALS: 4 tongue depressors for each child
White construction paper
Red construction paper
Black construction paper
Gold foil
White pipe cleaner
Red and black tempera

DIRECTIONS: Paint 2 tongue depressors black and the other 2 red. Let dry. Cut jacket from red construction paper. Cut circles from gold foil for buttons. Glue on red jacket. Cut pipe cleaner into 3 pieces, long enough to connect the buttons. Bend each pipe cleaner slightly and glue as in illustration. Glue ends of black tongue depressors behind red jacket, to represent legs. Break part of red tongue depressors so they are shorter to represent arms. Glue on back of jacket. Cut face from white construction paper. Cut hat, as well as facial features, from black construction paper. Glue in appropriate places. Glue on head to complete soldier.

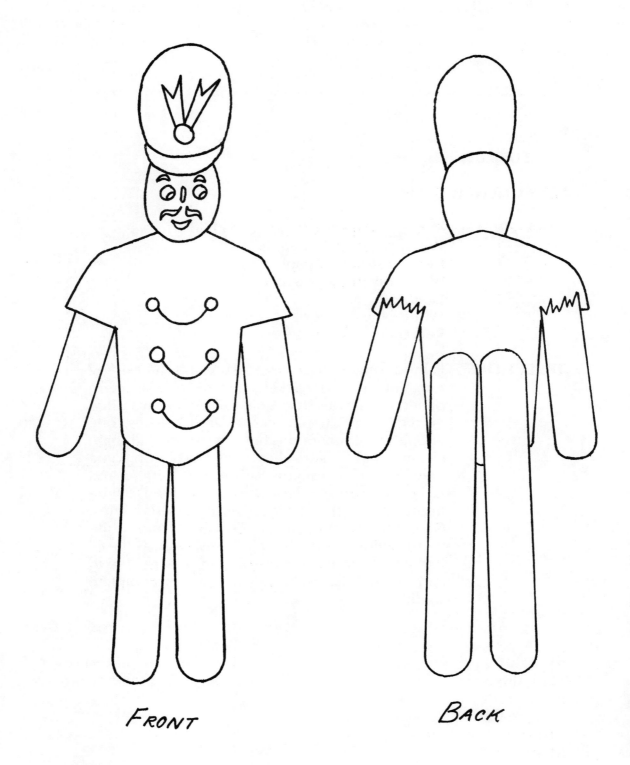

FRONT   BACK

Patriotic #1

DIRECTIONS: We have a great country and have had some great men as President. See if you know some of them by solving this crossword puzzle.

ACROSS

1. Our first president
2. Abbreviation for advertisement
4. Opposite of *yes*
7. An Indian name for king
12. He was president for 2 terms.
13. The first three letters of *small*
14. Myself
15. Opposite of *off*
16. Initials for Lyndon Johnson
17. This president's last name means, "To make a hole through."
19. Martin Van _____
20. A plural ending

DOWN

1. It happens when countries don't get along
3. The president after Washington
5. Inside
6. After his twelfth year, a child becomes a _ _ _ _
8. The first president to resign
9. Initials for Abraham Lincoln
10. Eaten with bread
11. A girl's name
14. His first name was James
15. Single
18. Initials for Dwight Eisenhower
19. A bolt
21. Therefore

Patriotic #2

Using each verse,
only letter can
the no you
letters more make
in often the
the than names
verse it of
below appears five
and in American
using the Presidents?

"Obey the government, for
God is the one who has put
it there."

Romans 13:1

1. He was the first President of the United States.

   ___ ___ ___ ___ ___ ___ ___ ___ ___ ___

2. This man was elected as President for two consecutive terms.

   ___ ___ ___ ___ ___

3. This President's first name was Warren.

   ___ ___ ___ ___ ___ ___ ___

4. This man was President just before Franklin D. Roosevelt.

   ___ ___ ___ ___ ___ ___

5. He was the 9th President's grandson and became our twenty-third President.

   ___ ___ ___ ___ ___ ___ ___ ___

August

While the earth remaineth,
seedtime and
harvest,
and
cold and heat,
and
summer
and
winter,
and day and night
shall not cease.
Genesis 8:22

Summer Gold

The hills are decked with gold nuggets
As summer puts on her display.
Bright dandelions break through the earth
And seem to appear in a day.

Roadsides glisten with yellow
Like a million suns in the grass,
And children can have all the gold
By gathering when they pass.

—Norma Reeser

SUBJECT: Summer

ART ACTIVITY: Turtle

MATERIALS: One egg cup from egg carton
Green construction paper
Green and brown tempera
Markers
Paintbrushes

DIRECTIONS: Paint egg cup green. Let dry.
Then paint spots on turtle. Cut head,
legs and tail from green construction
paper. Use marker to draw eyes. Glue
head, legs and tail in appropriate
places.

ART ACTIVITY: Bee

MATERIALS: Yellow, black and white tempera
2 paper fasteners for each child
Yellow pipe cleaner
White construction paper
Scissors
Paintbrushes
Egg carton

DIRECTIONS: Cut 3 egg cup section from egg carton. Paint
yellow stripes on egg carton. Let dry. Then paint
white spots for eyes. When dry, paint rest of bee
and part of eyes black. Let dry. Cut wings from
white construction paper. Attach wings to bee
with paper fasteners. Insert pipe cleaner for
antennae.

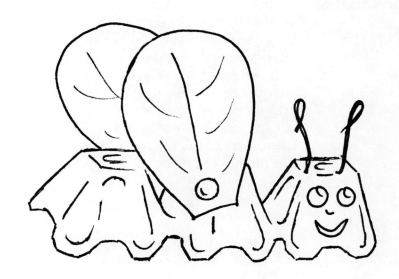

SUBJECT: Summer

ART ACTIVITY: Boat mobile

MATERIALS: 2, 9″ x 10″ pieces blue construction paper
2, 2″ squares black construction paper
18″ piece of yarn
Scissors
Glue

DIRECTIONS: A pattern can be made for each child (see illustration), if desired. The child cuts 2 boats from the 9″ x 10″ paper. Cut middle out as in illustration. Holding the 2″ square pieces together, cut them into an anchor. Place yarn between the two anchors, and glue the two pieces together. Place the anchor in the center of the cut-out middle, leaving enough yarn so it will hang in the center. Glue yarn between the two boat pieces and glue the pieces together.

Summer #1

If you cross out every third letter, you will find the verses from Job 37:14,17 (The Living Bible)

```
S  T  R  O  P  Q  A  N  J  D  C  X  O  N
T  S  I  A  D  E  B  R  T  A  H  E  O  W
O  E  N  D  U  E  R  K  F  U  M  L  M  F
I  R  D  A  C  S  L  E  H  S  O  N  F  G
P  O  D  T  .  .  .  D  O  R  Y  O  T  U
K  O  N  O  L  W  W  I  H  Y  V  Y  O  E
U  B  S  E  C  T  O  M  O  E  W  E  A  R
A  M  W  N  H  E  C  N  T  A  H  E  B  S
O  C  U  T  D  H  W  E  I  N  F  D  I  G
S  B  H  L  O  I  W  I  J  N  G  K?
```

108

DIRECTIONS: There are some scrambled words in the verse below. Unscramble them and use those letters which will be in the frames after unscrambling the words to form a season of the year.

God made two huge ¹ s t l g h i, the ² n u s and the ³ o n o m, to shine down upon the earth—the larger one, the sun, to preside over the day and the ⁴ l s m e a l r one ⁵ h e t moon to ⁶ d i e s e r p through the night; he also made the stars. Genesis 1:16, LB

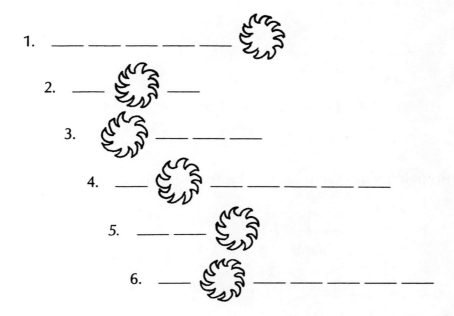

Answers to Activity Sheets

Answers to Activity Sheets

Rosh Hashana #1: Rosh Hashana is the Jewish New Year.

#2: **F**irst Fruits
P**E**ntecost
Pa**S**sover
Trumpets
Israel
Unlea**V**ened Bread
Day of **A**tonement
Tabernac**L**es

Autumn #1: **A**ngels
Upright
Trust
Uphold
Mercies
Needy

#2: Fall, fell, dell, deal, deaf, leaf

Thanksgiving #1: We ought to be thankful for all things.

#2: Mayflower, turkey, Plymouth, harvest, Thursday, religion.
"Giving *t h a n k s* always for all things."

Christmas #1: 1. Jesus 2. Mary 3. Joseph 4. Herod
5. Frankincense 6. Inn 7. Christ
8. Star 9. Gold 10. Shepherd

#2: 1. Behold, Christ entered humbly into our sinful, uninviting, vile world.
2. Angels came, heavenly hosts sang.
3. Come let us worship.
4. Adore Christ, our Savior today.
1. Welcome today, the Savior of all.
2. You received God's gift.
3. Rejoice, the Son of God is born.

Winter #1: For he directs the snow, the showers, and storm to fall upon the earth. Job 37:6 (Living Bible)

#2: Do you know how God controls all nature? Have you visited the treasuries of the snow? Job 37:15; 38:22 (Living Bible)

Valentine #1: Love

#2:

GIVE	LOVE	KIND	CARD
IDEA	OPEN	IDEA	AREA
VEER	VEND	NEAR	READ
EARN	ENDS	DARE	DADS

Spring #1: All things bright and beautiful
All creatures great and small
All things wise and wonderful
The Lord God made them all.

#2: spring, grow, warbler, rain, newness, song, grass, scene, Eden, nest, thrush.

Easter #1: (1) risen (2) Cleopas (3) denied (4) tomb
(5) Joanna (6) Mary (7) Sabbath (8) ointment
(9) women (10) rolled (11) robber (12) cross

#2: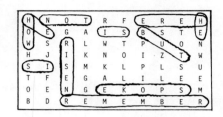

Mother's Day #1: Children, obey your parents.

#2: Mary, Orpah, Tabitha, Hannah, Eve, Rachel

Father's Day #1: Joseph, Jacob, Isaac, Adam, David, Abraham, Moses, Jairus, Job, Noah.

#2: Gene, Josh, Sam, Dan, Tim, Jon, Les, Joe, Ron, Philip.

Patriotic #1:

Across		
1. Washington	17. Pierce	6. Teen
2. Ad	19. Buren	8. Nixon
4. No	20. Es	9. AL
7. Raja		10. Jam
12. Madison		11. Ada
13. Sma		14. Monroe
14. Me	Down	15. One
15. On	1. War	18. DE
16. LJ	3. Adams	19. Bar
	5. In	21. So

#2: 1. Washington, 2. Monroe, 3. Harding, 4. Hoover, 5. Harrison

Summer #1: Stop and consider the wonderful miracles of God. Do you know why you become warm when the south wind is blowing? Job 37:14, 17 (Living Bible)

#2: (1) Lights (2) Sun (3) Moon (4) Smaller (5) The (6) Preside   SUMMER

112